MIND MATTERS

Confronting America's Mental
Health Crisis

BY

DR. ELVIRA S. GRAVES

TABLE OF CONTENTS

Disclaimer

copyright@ © by Dr. Elvira S. Graves 2024.
All rights reserved.
Before this document is duplicated or reproduced in any manner, the publisher's consent must be gained. Therefore, the contents within can neither be stored electronically, transferred, nor kept in a database. Neither in part nor full can the document be copied, scanned, faxed, or retained without approval from the publisher or creator.

Introduction:

The Unseen Epidemic

The landscape of mental health in America today is one of silent struggle and unseen challenges. In recent years, the nation has witnessed a steady increase in mental health issues, with current statistics painting a stark picture of widespread affliction. As reported by Mental Health America, an estimated **19.86%** of adults are grappling with mental illness, translating to nearly **50 million Americans**. Among these, **4.91%** are enduring severe mental illness, which significantly disrupts their daily functioning. To truly grasp the magnitude of this crisis, we must delve into its prevalence and profound impact on society. Mental health disorders encompass a broad spectrum of conditions, from generalized anxiety and major depressive disorders to more debilitating illnesses like schizophrenia and bipolar disorder. The repercussions of these conditions are extensive, affecting individuals' capacity to work, sustain relationships, and engage in community life.

The crisis is further illuminated through personal stories that offer a window into the lived experiences of those battling mental health conditions. These narratives are not merely anecdotes but testaments to the resilience and fortitude of individuals navigating the complexities of their mental well-being. They underscore the critical need for accessible, quality mental health care and support systems.

Several societal factors contribute to America's mental health crisis, including:

- **Limited Access to Care**: Many individuals face barriers such as a shortage of service providers, cultural and language barriers, high costs of care, lack of health insurance, and stigma associated with seeking help.
- **Economic Stress**: Economic uncertainty and stress, similar to levels reported during the 2008 recession, have been significant sources of stress for many Americans.
- **Public Health Emergencies**: The coronavirus pandemic has been a substantial source of stress, with nearly 78% of adults citing it as a significant stressor.
- **Social Inequality**: Issues like police violence toward minorities and discrimination have been

reported as significant sources of stress across various demographics.

- **Global Threats**: Social and economic inequalities, war, and climate crises are global structural threats that have exacerbated mental health issues. Depression and anxiety increased by more than 25% in the first year of the pandemic alone.
- **Social Media and Isolation**: The psychological impacts of social media platforms contribute to conditions of isolation, anxiety, and depression.

These factors collectively create a challenging environment for mental well-being, necessitating a multifaceted approach to address the crisis effectively. As we delve deeper into confronting America's mental health crisis, it is imperative to acknowledge that each statistic represents a human being with a unique story of endurance and hope. By bringing these stories to the forefront, we aim to dismantle the stigma that shrouds mental health and advocate for a future where comprehensive care, empathy, and understanding are not just ideals but realities.

Chapter 1: Stigma and Silence

In "Mind Matters: Confronting America's Mental Health Crisis," we embark on a journey to dismantle the barriers of stigma and silence that have long plagued the conversation around mental health. Chapter 1, "Stigma and Silence," lays the foundation for understanding the deep-seated prejudices that hinder open dialogue and acceptance. Within these pages, we begin to unravel the complex tapestry of misconceptions, tracing the threads back to their historical and cultural origins.

Understanding Stigma: Origins and Consequences
Stigma, derived from the Greek word for 'mark' or 'brand,' historically signified a physical sign of disgrace. In the context of mental health, stigma manifests as a

mark of shame, leading to discrimination against those with mental illness. This section will explore how stigma has evolved, from ancient beliefs that linked mental illness to supernatural causes, to the medieval era where asylums became places of fear and isolation. In modern times, stigma is often perpetuated by media portrayals that equate mental illness with violence or instability. Movies like "Psycho" and "One Flew Over the Cuckoo's Nest" have left indelible marks on the public psyche, creating enduring stereotypes. The consequences of such stigma are profound: individuals may avoid seeking help for fear of being labeled or ostracized, leading to untreated conditions and worsening symptoms.

The origins of mental health stigma are as old as human society itself. In ancient civilizations, mental illness was often attributed to supernatural forces or divine punishment. For instance, in ancient Greece, it was believed that mental illness could be a result of displeasure from the gods. In medieval Europe, it was commonly associated with witchcraft or possession by evil spirits. These beliefs led to fear and exclusion of individuals with mental health issues.

As medical science advanced, the understanding of mental illness began to shift towards a biological perspective. However, the stigma persisted, now rooted in a fear of the unknown and the unpredictable nature of mental health conditions. The establishment of asylums in the 18th and 19th centuries aimed to provide care but often resulted in further isolation and mistreatment, reinforcing negative perceptions. In the 20th century, with the advent of psychology and psychiatry, there was hope for stigmatization. Yet, sensationalized media portrayals and a lack of public education continued to feed the cycle of fear and misunderstanding. It wasn't until the latter half of the century that movements began to emerge, challenging these misconceptions and advocating for the rights and dignity of those affected by mental illness.

The consequences of this long history of stigma are far-reaching. Individuals may internalize these negative attitudes, leading to self-stigma and a reluctance to seek help or adhere to treatment. This can result in a cascade of negative outcomes including social isolation, worsening mental health conditions, and even suicide. Understanding this history is crucial for dismantling stigma. It allows us to see how deeply ingrained these attitudes are in our culture and provides a framework for developing strategies to combat them. By learning from the past, we can build a more compassionate and informed future where mental health is treated with the same seriousness and empathy as physical health.

Breaking the Silence: Advocacy and Awareness Campaigns

The silence surrounding mental health is deafening, but it is being challenged by voices that refuse to be muted. Advocacy groups have emerged as champions for change, leveraging awareness campaigns to educate the public and dispel myths. This section will highlight key initiatives like 'Time to Change' and 'Mental Health America,' which have significantly shifted public perception.

The Role of Media and Culture in Perpetuating Stigma

Media and culture play a pivotal role in shaping public perception. Unfortunately, they have often contributed to the stigma surrounding mental health. From news reports that disproportionately link mental illness with violence, to films and TV shows that depict those with mental health issues as dangerous or comical, the media has a history of reinforcing negative stereotypes. This portrayal can lead to a culture of fear and misunderstanding, where people with mental illness are seen as 'other' or less than others. Cultural narratives also play a part. In many societies, there is an expectation to be strong and self-reliant, and admitting to mental health struggles can be seen as a weakness. This can prevent people from speaking out or seeking help.

The media can help change this narrative by highlighting stories of recovery and resilience, showing that mental health issues are common and treatable.

Personal Stories of Stigma and Its Impact on Individuals

Personal stories have the power to humanize the issue of mental health stigma. By sharing their experiences, individuals can highlight the real world impact of stigma. For example, someone might share how they were afraid to disclose their depression at work for fear of losing their job, or how they were treated differently by friends and family after a diagnosis of bipolar disorder.

These stories can be heart-wrenching but also inspiring. They show the courage it takes to confront stigma and can motivate others to act with more empathy and understanding. Including such narratives in your book will provide readers with a personal connection to the issue and illustrate the urgent need for change.

The Consequences of Stigma on Mental Health Treatment and Recovery

Stigma not only affects individuals socially but also has serious implications for treatment and recovery. It can lead to delays in seeking help, misdiagnosis, and inadequate treatment. Stigma can also affect funding for mental health services and research, leading to fewer resources for those in need.

Recovery from mental illness is possible, but it requires a supportive environment free from judgment. Stigma creates barriers that can make recovery more difficult. By addressing stigma, we can improve access to care, enhance the quality of treatment, and support recovery efforts. These campaigns employ various strategies, from celebrity endorsements to grassroots community outreach, aiming to normalize conversations about mental health. Social media has become invaluable in this fight, providing platforms for individuals to share their stories and connect with others. The success of these campaigns can be measured not just in increased awareness but in tangible changes in policy and practice.

Media Portrayal of Mental Illness
The media's portrayal of mental illness has a profound impact on public perception and stigma. Historically, the media has often depicted mental illness through a lens of fear, misunderstanding, and sensationalism. This portrayal can take various forms:

Movies and Television

Films and TV shows have frequently used mental illness as a plot device, often portraying characters with mental health issues as violent, unpredictable, or fundamentally flawed. For instance, the character of Norman Bates in Alfred Hitchcock's "Psycho" is often cited as an example of how mental illness can be linked to violence in the public imagination. Similarly, the portrayal of characters in psychiatric hospitals, such as in "One Flew Over the Cuckoo's Nest," has contributed to a fear and misunderstanding of these institutions.

News Media

The news media also plays a role in perpetuating stigma. Reports on mental illness often emerge in the context of violent incidents, creating an association between mental illness and danger in the public mind. This coverage can be one-sided and lacks depth, failing to provide a balanced view that includes the experiences of the majority of individuals with mental health issues who live peaceful and productive lives.

Social Media

With the rise of social media, there is an opportunity for more nuanced and personal portrayals of mental illness. However, social media can also be a double-edged sword; while it allows individuals to share their stories and build supportive communities, it can also spread misinformation and harmful stereotypes.

The Impact

These portrayals can lead to widespread misconceptions about mental illness, making individuals reluctant to discuss their mental health issues or seek help. They can also influence public policy and healthcare funding decisions, often to the detriment of mental health services.

Moving Forward

To combat these negative portrayals, the media need to strive for accuracy and sensitivity when depicting mental illness. This includes consulting with mental health professionals and individuals with lived experience to ensure truthful and respectful representations. Additionally, highlighting stories of recovery and success can help to balance the narrative and show that having a mental illness is just one part of a person's life.

Here are some examples of positive portrayals of mental health in the media:

Movies and Television
- **"Silver Linings Playbook"** - This film portrays mental illness with nuance and empathy, focusing on a man's journey to manage his bipolar disorder. It highlights themes of recovery, the importance of support systems, and the possibility of finding love and fulfillment despite mental health challenges.

- **"A Beautiful Mind"** - Based on the true story of John Nash, a Nobel Laureate in Economics who lived with schizophrenia, this movie depicts the challenges and triumphs of living with a mental illness, emphasizing Nash's brilliance and resilience.

Television Shows
- **"This Is Us"** - This series has been praised for its sensitive portrayal of anxiety and depression, particularly through the character Randall Pearson. It shows his struggles realistically but also emphasizes his strength and the support he receives from his family.
- "BoJack Horseman" is an animated show that doesn't shy away from exploring themes of depression, addiction, and self-worth. It's been commended for its honest and often heartbreakingly accurate depiction of these issues.

News Media
- Features on Mental Health Advocates - News outlets have increasingly featured stories of individuals who advocate for mental health awareness, such as Olympic swimmer Michael Phelps discussing his battle with depression or actress Taraji P. Henson speaking about her efforts to destigmatize mental illness.

Social Media Campaigns
- BellLetsTalk - An annual social media campaign encouraging open conversations about mental health and raising funds for mental health initiatives. It has helped to break down barriers and promote understanding through personal stories shared online.

As we transition into breaking the silence, we spotlight the valiant efforts of advocacy groups that have risen to challenge the status quo. Campaigns like 'Bring Change to Mind' and 'NAMI's StigmaFree' pledge to change perceptions one story at a time. We dissect these movements to understand what makes them resonate with people, drawing lessons from their triumphs and setbacks. This chapter is an examination and a call to action—a beacon for those silenced by stigma to find their voice. With every page, we aim to empower readers with knowledge, compassion, and courage to confront America's mental health crisis head-on.

Chapter 2: The Spectrum of Mental Disorders

Mental disorders are defined as syndromes characterized by clinically significant disturbances in an individual's cognition, emotional regulation, or behavior. These disturbances reflect a dysfunction in psychological, biological, or developmental processes underlying mental functioning. They are usually associated with significant distress or disability in social, occupational, or other important activities.

The Concept of a Spectrum and Its Significance

The term 'spectrum' in mental health acknowledges that there is not a one-size-fits-all approach to understanding mental disorders. Instead, it suggests a range or continuum of symptoms and behaviors, with varying degrees of severity and impact on daily life. This concept is significant because it allows for a more personalized understanding of each individual's experience with mental illness, rather than categorizing all individuals under rigid diagnostic labels.

Categories of Mental Disorders
Mental disorders can be broadly categorized into several groups:

- **Mood Disorders:** These include conditions like depression and bipolar disorder, where the primary symptom is a disturbance in mood.
- **Anxiety Disorders**: This category encompasses disorders characterized by excessive fear and anxiety, such as generalized anxiety disorder, panic disorder, and phobias.
- **Psychotic Disorders:** Disorders like schizophrenia fall into this category, where individuals may experience delusions, hallucinations, and disorganized thinking.
- **Personality Disorders**: These are characterized by enduring patterns of behavior and inner experiences that deviate markedly from the expectations of the individual's culture.
- **Eating Disorders:** Conditions such as anorexia nervosa and bulimia nervosa are included here, where there is an obsession with food and body weight.
- **Trauma- and Stressor-Related Disorders**: These include post-traumatic stress disorder (PTSD) and acute

stress disorder, which occur as a response to a traumatic or stressful event.

Common mental disorders with relevant examples:
Depression: Depression is a mood disorder characterized by persistent feelings of sadness, hopelessness, and a lack of interest or pleasure in activities. It can lead to various emotional and physical problems and can decrease a person's ability to function at work and at home. For example, a person with depression may experience significant weight loss, insomnia, and a diminished ability to think or concentrate.

Anxiety Disorders: Anxiety disorders involve more than temporary worry or fear. For a person with an anxiety disorder, the anxiety does not go away and can get worse over time. Symptoms can interfere with daily activities such as job performance, schoolwork, and relationships. For instance, someone with generalized anxiety disorder might have excessive, ongoing worry that interferes with daily activities.

Bipolar Disorder: Bipolar disorder is characterized by dramatic shifts in mood, energy, and activity levels that affect a person's ability to carry out day-to-day tasks. These shifts can range from highs (mania or hypomania) to lows (depression). An example is a person experiencing episodes of high energy and activity (manic episodes) and then suddenly feeling tired and depressed (depressive episodes).

Schizophrenia: Schizophrenia is a serious mental disorder in which people interpret reality abnormally. It may result in some combination of hallucinations, delusions, and extremely disordered thinking and behavior. An illustrative case would be a person hearing voices that are not there (auditory hallucinations) or believing that others are controlling their thoughts (delusion of control).

Less Common Mental Disorders

Dissociative Disorders: These disorders involve disconnection and lack of continuity between thoughts, memories, surroundings, actions, and identity. For example, dissociative identity disorder (formerly known as multiple personality disorder) involves the presence of two or more distinct personality states.

Eating Disorders: Eating disorders are characterized by obsessive concerns with weight and disruptive eating patterns that negatively impact physical and mental health. Anorexia nervosa is an example where an individual has an intense fear of gaining weight and severely restricts food intake.

Personality Disorders: Personality disorders are characterized by enduring patterns of behavior, cognition, and inner experience that deviate markedly

from the expectations of the individual's culture. Borderline personality
disorder, for instance, involves patterns of instability in interpersonal relationships, self-image, and affect, along with marked impulsivity.

Childhood-Onset Mental Disorders
- Autism Spectrum Disorder (ASD)

ASD is a developmental disorder that affects communication and behavior. For example, a child with ASD might have difficulty understanding social cues and may engage in repetitive behaviors.

- Attention Deficit Hyperactivity Disorder (ADHD)

ADHD is characterized by patterns of inattention, hyperactivity, and impulsivity. A child with ADHD may struggle to focus on tasks, sit still, or wait their turn in activities.

-Learning Disorders

These disorders affect a child's ability to receive and process information. Dyslexia is an example where a child has difficulties with accurate or fluent word recognition and poor spelling and decoding abilities.

The Impact of Mental Disorders
On Individuals

Mental disorders can lead to personal suffering, decreased quality of life, and loss of independence. For instance, an individual with severe depression may be unable to maintain employment or relationships.

On Families and Relationships

Mental disorders can put a strain on family systems and relationships. A family might experience stress and conflict due to the behavioral challenges of a member with bipolar disorder.

On Society

The societal impact includes economic costs related to healthcare services, lost productivity, and the need for social support systems. For example, society must provide resources for individuals with schizophrenia who may require long-term care. Recognizing the spectrum of mental disorders is essential for empathy and effective support. This chapter underscores the importance of awareness and education in fostering a more inclusive society.

Chapter 3: Vulnerable Populations

Mental Health in Children and Adolescents.

Mental health issues are increasingly recognized in children and adolescents. For example, studies show that up to 20% of children worldwide may have a mental health problem. Conditions like anxiety disorders, behavior disorders, and mood disorders are common among young people.

Impact of Mental Health on Development and Education

Mental health issues can significantly affect a child's development and educational attainment. A child with ADHD may struggle with executive functions like planning and organization, impacting their academic performance. Similarly, a teenager with depression might experience social withdrawal and a lack of motivation, affecting both their schoolwork and personal development.

Challenges in Diagnosis and Treatment

Diagnosing mental health issues in young people can be challenging due to the natural changes that occur during growth. Moreover, there's often a stigma associated with mental health that can prevent families from seeking help. Treatment challenges include a shortage of child psychiatrists and psychologists, as well as the need for age-appropriate therapies.

The Elderly and Mental Health Challenges

Common Mental Health Conditions in Older Adults

Older adults often face mental health challenges such as depression, anxiety, and dementia. For instance, late-life depression affects approximately 6 million Americans aged 65 and older, but only 10% receive treatment.

The Role of Comorbidities and Aging-Related Changes

Comorbidities like heart disease or diabetes can exacerbate mental health issues in the elderly. Aging-related changes, such as cognitive decline or the loss of loved ones, can also contribute to mental health conditions. For example, an older adult with mobility issues may experience isolation, leading to depression.

Barriers to Accessing Mental Health Care
Many older adults face barriers to accessing mental health care, including stigma, transportation difficulties, and a lack of awareness about mental health services. Additionally, there's a shortage of geriatric mental health professionals, which can delay diagnosis and treatment.

Minority Mental Health Disparities
The Impact of Cultural, Social, and Economic Factors on Mental Health
Cultural stigma, social discrimination, and economic inequality can significantly impact the mental health of minority groups. For example, African Americans are 20% more likely to experience serious mental health problems than the general population, partly due to unaddressed social determinants of health like poverty and discrimination.
Specific Challenges Faced by Minority Groups
Minority groups often face challenges such as language barriers, mistrust in the healthcare system, and a lack of culturally competent care providers. For instance, Hispanic individuals may avoid seeking mental health care due to language barriers or fear of deportation.

Strategies to Address Disparities and Improve Access to Care

Strategies include increasing cultural competence among healthcare providers, improving language access services, and implementing community-based interventions. For example, the use of community health workers who share the cultural background of the populations they serve has been effective in improving access to mental health care. The chapter will conclude by stressing the need for targeted efforts to understand and mitigate the unique challenges faced by minority populations in accessing mental health care. It will call for an inclusive approach that considers cultural nuances and promotes equity in mental health outcomes.

Chapter 4: Barriers to Treatment

Access to Mental Health Care

Access to mental health services varies greatly depending on where one lives. In urban areas, there might be a higher concentration of mental health professionals, but the demand for services can lead to long waiting lists. For example, in New York City, it's not uncommon for individuals to wait several weeks or even months for an appointment with a psychiatrist. In contrast, rural areas often face a scarcity of mental health services. Residents might have to travel long distances to see a mental health provider if there are any available at all. For instance, in rural Wyoming, there are only 5.75 mental health professionals per 10,000 people, compared to the national average of 28.4. The shortage of mental health professionals exacerbates these geographic disparities. With fewer professionals entering the field and an aging workforce retiring, many areas are left with insufficient care. This shortage impacts treatment options and quality of care; patients may have limited access to specialized treatments or may be seen less frequently than needed for effective care.

The Cost of Mental Health Treatment
The financial aspect of mental health care can be a significant barrier for many. Treatments for mental health conditions, such as therapy sessions, medication, and hospitalization, can be expensive, and not all are covered by insurance. For example, cognitive-behavioral therapy (CBT), a common and effective treatment for conditions like depression and anxiety, can cost between $100 to $200 per session without insurance. Insurance coverage plays a crucial role in accessing mental health care. While some insurance plans offer comprehensive mental health benefits, others may have limited coverage with high deductibles or copays. This can leave patients with substantial out-of-pocket expenses, making it difficult for those with lower incomes to afford ongoing treatment. To illustrate, consider the case of a single parent earning a modest income who is diagnosed with bipolar disorder. The cost of their medication and bi-weekly therapy sessions may amount to several hundred dollars a month – a significant portion of their budget. Without adequate insurance coverage, they

might have to choose between essential expenses and their mental health treatment.

Cultural Barriers and Misconceptions

Cultural beliefs and stigma are powerful forces that can prevent individuals from seeking mental health treatment. In many cultures, mental illness may be seen as a sign of weakness or a lack of moral character. For example, in some Asian communities, the concept of "saving face" can lead individuals to hide their mental health struggles to avoid humiliating their families. Misconceptions about mental illness also contribute to these barriers. Common myths, such as the belief that mental health issues can be overcome by willpower alone or that they are not as serious as physical health issues, can diminish the perceived need for professional treatment. This is evident in the way some people dismiss depression as just feeling sad and encourage those suffering to simply "cheer up." To address these cultural barriers and misconceptions, systemic changes are needed. This includes increasing public awareness about mental health, integrating mental health education into school curricula, and promoting culturally sensitive care within the healthcare system.

The chapter concludes by underscoring the importance of dismantling cultural barriers and correcting misconceptions to improve access to mental health care. It calls for a collective effort to create a society where mental health is valued just as much as physical health, ensuring that all individuals have the support they need.

Chapter 5: The Role of Healthcare Providers

Training and Education for Providers
Specialized training in mental health is essential for healthcare providers to identify, understand, and treat mental health conditions effectively. For instance, primary care physicians who receive training in recognizing symptoms of depression are more likely to diagnose it accurately and provide appropriate referrals or treatment. Programs like Mental Health First Aid (MHFA) train providers across various healthcare settings to better understand and respond to signs of mental illnesses and substance use disorders. This program has been widely adopted and is credited with improving participants' knowledge of mental disorders, reducing stigma, and increasing supportive actions toward individuals with mental health conditions. Another example is the integration of psychiatric education into nursing programs, equipping nurses with the skills to offer mental health support in a range of clinical settings. Initiatives like these highlight the

growing recognition of the importance of mental health training in providing comprehensive care.

Integrating Mental Health into Primary Care

Incorporating mental health screenings and treatments into primary care settings can lead to early detection and intervention, which are crucial for effective treatment outcomes. For example, routine depression screenings during primary care visits have been shown to increase the diagnosis and treatment of this condition, leading to better patient outcomes. A notable case study is the IMPACT (Improving Mood-Promoting Access to Collaborative Treatment) program, which integrates depression treatment into primary care for older adults. This program has demonstrated significant improvements in depressive symptoms, physical functioning, and quality of life compared to usual care. Another example is the Collaborative Care Model, where primary care providers work closely with care managers and psychiatric consultants to treat common mental health conditions. Studies have shown that this model leads to better care, improved patient outcomes, and lower costs.

Ethical Considerations in Treatment

Healthcare providers often navigate complex ethical dilemmas in mental health treatment. Patient confidentiality is paramount, yet there are situations, such as when a patient poses a risk to themselves or others, where breaching confidentiality may be necessary to prevent harm.

For example, consider the case of a therapist who learns that their patient is contemplating serious harm to another person. The therapist must weigh the ethical obligation of confidentiality against the duty to protect potential victims, which may require disclosing information to authorities. Informed consent is another critical ethical consideration. Patients must understand their treatment options and the associated risks and benefits to make informed decisions about their care. This can be challenging when working with patients experiencing severe mental health issues that may impair their decision-making capacity. A real-world example is when a patient with severe schizophrenia is recommended for a new medication regimen. The healthcare provider must ensure that the patient comprehensively understands the potential side effects and benefits of the medication, despite their cognitive challenges.

The chapter concludes by emphasizing the importance of comprehensive training in ethics for healthcare providers. It advocates for the integration of services and ethical mindfulness to enhance the quality and accessibility of mental health care, ensuring that patients receive effective and ethically sound treatment.

Chapter 6: Innovative Therapies and Treatments

This chapter will explore the cutting-edge advancements in mental health treatments, from new psychotherapy techniques to personalized medicine and alternative therapies.

Advances in Psychotherapy

Psychotherapy has seen remarkable advancements with the integration of technology. Virtual reality exposure therapy (VRET) is one such development that has transformed the treatment of conditions like PTSD. By immersing patients in a controlled virtual environment, therapists can safely expose them to their trauma triggers, helping them learn to cope in a safe space. Research has shown VRET to be as effective as traditional exposure therapy for PTSD, with the added benefit of being more engaging for patients. Digital therapeutics, another innovative approach, involves using digital systems—often mobile apps—to deliver evidence-based therapeutic interventions. For example, apps that use cognitive-behavioral therapy (CBT) principles have been developed to help users manage anxiety and depression symptoms. These apps are effective in reducing symptoms and are particularly useful for people who may not have access to traditional in-person therapy.

Psychopharmacology and Personalized Medicine
The field of psychopharmacology is evolving with the advent of personalized medicine, particularly through genetic testing. Pharmacogenomics, the study of how genes affect a person's response to drugs, is increasingly being used to tailor psychiatric medication prescriptions. For instance, genetic tests can predict how patients might metabolize certain antidepressants, helping to avoid medications that could cause adverse effects or be less effective. Looking ahead, brain stimulation techniques like transcranial magnetic stimulation (TMS) and deep brain stimulation (DBS) are at the forefront of treatment innovation. TMS uses magnetic fields to stimulate nerve cells in the brain to improve symptoms of depression, while DBS involves implanting electrodes in specific

areas of the brain to regulate abnormal impulses. Both techniques have shown promise in treating conditions that have not responded to traditional therapies.

Personalized medicine in mental health, while promising, raises several ethical considerations:

Privacy and Confidentiality: Genetic testing for personalized medicine involves sensitive personal information that must be protected. There are concerns about who has access to this data and how it might be used, potentially affecting insurance coverage and employment opportunities.

Informed Consent: Patients must fully understand the implications of genetic testing, including the potential for discovering incidental findings unrelated to their mental health treatment.

Equity: There's a risk that personalized medicine could exacerbate healthcare disparities if these advanced treatments are not accessible to all segments of the population.

Expectations: While genetic testing can provide valuable information, it's not a definitive solution. Managing patient expectations regarding the effectiveness of personalized treatments is crucial.

These ethical implications require careful consideration to ensure that the benefits of personalized medicine are realized without compromising patient rights and equity in healthcare.

Alternative and Complementary Therapies
The interest in alternative and complementary therapies for mental health has surged, with mindfulness-based stress reduction (MBSR) and yoga being prominent examples. MBSR is a structured program that combines mindfulness meditation and yoga to reduce stress. It has been widely studied and shown to be effective in reducing symptoms of anxiety and depression. Yoga, which incorporates physical postures, breathing exercises, and meditation, has also gained attention for its mental health benefits. Research indicates that yoga can improve mood and may be as effective as antidepressants in treating depression.

For instance, a study published in the Journal of Alternative and Complementary Medicine found that participants who completed an eight-week MBSR program showed significant reductions in anxiety and depression scores compared to a control group. Similarly, a randomized controlled trial reported in the Journal of Clinical Psychiatry observed that yoga participants had lower levels of depression after three months compared to those who did not practice yoga.

This chapter has highlighted the exciting advancements in mental health treatment, from the integration of technology in psychotherapy to the personalization of psychopharmacology and the embrace of alternative therapies. These innovations offer a glimpse into a future where mental health care is more accessible, effective, and tailored to individual needs. As we continue to explore and validate these new approaches, it's crucial to consider the ethical implications and strive for equity in access to these treatments. The potential of these therapies to revolutionize care is immense, promising a new era of hope and healing for patients with mental health conditions.

Chapter 7: Community and Support

This chapter delves into the critical role that community support plays in mental health care, examining how support groups, non-profit organizations, and family involvement contribute to recovery and well-being.

The Power of Support Groups and Peer Networks
Support groups and peer networks play a vital role in mental health care by providing a platform for shared experiences and mutual support. These groups offer a sense of belonging, reduce isolation, and can significantly improve coping strategies. For example, Alcoholics Anonymous (AA) is a well-known support group that has helped countless individuals overcome addiction through a structured program and the support of peers who have faced similar challenges. The success of AA has led to the formation of other peer-led groups for various mental health conditions. Another inspiring story is that of a peer support network for veterans dealing with PTSD, where members share their

experiences and offer each other emotional support. This network has been instrumental in helping veterans reintegrate into civilian life and manage their symptoms more effectively. These examples demonstrate the profound impact that support groups and peer networks can have on individuals' lives, offering hope and practical assistance to those navigating mental health challenges.

Role of Nonprofits and Community Organizations
Nonprofits and community organizations are essential in the mental health landscape, offering resources, advocacy, and education to those in need. They fill gaps in the healthcare system, often providing services to underserved populations. For instance, NAMI (National Alliance on Mental Illness) is a non-profit organization that offers a variety of free programs, including education classes, support groups, and resources for individuals and families affected by mental illness. Their advocacy efforts have also led to policy changes that benefit the mental health community.

A case study worth noting is a community program that provided free mental health screenings and follow-up care in a rural area with limited access to psychiatric services. This program not only helped identify individuals with untreated mental health conditions but also connected them with necessary care, significantly improving the community's overall mental health. These examples underscore the critical role that nonprofits and community organizations play in supporting mental health care and advocating for necessary changes within the system.

Family Involvement in Mental Health Care
Family involvement can significantly influence treatment outcomes in mental health care. Supportive family members can provide emotional stability, encourage adherence to treatment plans, and help navigate the complexities of the healthcare system. For example, studies have shown that individuals with schizophrenia or bipolar disorder have better recovery rates when their families are involved in their care. Family education programs that teach coping strategies and communication skills can also improve the home environment for both the patient and family members. Guidance for families includes encouraging open communication, educating themselves about their mental health condition, and participating in therapy sessions when appropriate. It's also important for families to take care of their mental health, as caring for a loved one with a mental illness can be stressful.

This chapter has explored the indispensable role of community and support in mental health care. From support groups to non-profits and family involvement, it's clear that a strong support network can greatly enhance the well-being of those with mental health conditions. By fostering a more inclusive and supportive environment, we can collectively contribute to better mental health outcomes and a stronger, more resilient community.

Chapter 8: Policy and Advocacy

This chapter examines the landscape of mental health policy in the US, highlighting the importance of advocacy efforts in shaping these policies and presenting case studies of successful interventions.

Overview of Mental Health Policy in the US
The current state of mental health policy in the US is shaped by several key pieces of legislation, such as the Mental Health Parity and Addiction Equity Act (MHPAEA) and the Affordable Care Act (ACA), which have expanded coverage for mental health services. Funding for mental health programs comes from a combination of federal, state, and local sources, including Medicaid and the Substance Abuse and Mental Health Services Administration (SAMHSA).

Despite these policies, there are significant gaps in the system. Access to care remains a challenge, with many Americans living in areas with a shortage of mental health professionals. Stigma and lack of awareness also prevent people from seeking help. Moreover, funding is often inadequate to meet the demand for services, leading to long wait times and insufficient resources for preventive care. The criminal justice system also ends up being a de facto mental health provider due to a lack of community-based treatment options. Addressing these challenges requires a multifaceted approach that includes increasing funding for mental health services, expanding the workforce, and continuing to reduce stigma through education and awarcncss campaigns.

Advocacy Efforts for Policy Change
Individuals and organizations play a crucial role in influencing mental health policy through advocacy. Advocates work to raise awareness, lobby for increased funding, and push for legislative changes that can improve mental health care. For example, the "Bring Change to Mind" campaign, founded by actress Glenn Close, aims to end the stigma and discrimination surrounding mental illness. The campaign has been successful in sparking conversations and promoting understanding through public service announcements and school programs.

Another significant movement is the "Mental Health First Aid" program, which trains community members to recognize signs of mental health issues and provide initial help. This program has gained support from policymakers and has been implemented across various states, improving community response to mental health crises. These campaigns demonstrate the power of advocacy in driving policy change and enhancing the mental health care landscape.

Case Studies of Successful Policy Interventions
Several policies have had a significant positive impact on mental health care. For instance, the implementation of the 21st Century Cures Act has increased funding for mental health services and strengthened enforcement of mental health parity laws. A notable example is Oregon's "Unity Center for Behavioral Health," a policy intervention that created a collaborative care model integrating physical and mental health services. This center has reduced emergency room visits and improved patient outcomes by providing immediate psychiatric care. Factors contributing to the success of these policies include strong leadership, community involvement, and adequate funding. These elements ensure that policies are not only enacted but also effectively implemented.

This chapter has highlighted the pivotal role of policy and advocacy in advancing mental health care. Through informed and persistent efforts, advocates have achieved meaningful changes that provide better support for individuals with mental health conditions. These case studies serve as blueprints for future policy interventions, offering hope for continued progress in the field.

Chapter 9: Workplace Wellness

In today's fast-paced world, the workplace has become a critical setting for promoting mental health. This chapter explores the importance of mental health in the workplace, strategies employers can use to support their employees, and how to balance productivity with wellness.

Mental Health in the Workplace:
Mental health issues can significantly impact an employee's performance and overall well-being. Stress, anxiety, and depression are common in the workplace and can lead to decreased productivity, absenteeism, and higher healthcare costs. Creating a supportive work environment that recognizes mental health is essential for a healthy workforce.

Employer Strategies for Supporting Employee Mental Health:

Employers can adopt various strategies to support their employees' mental health. These include:

- Providing access to mental health resources such as Employee Assistance Programs (EAPs).
- Offering flexible work arrangements to help employees manage work-life balance.
- Implementing training programs for managers to recognize signs of mental distress and provide appropriate support

Balancing Productivity with Wellness:
Balancing productivity with wellness requires a shift in workplace culture. Employers should prioritize mental health as much as physical health. Encouraging regular breaks, promoting physical activity, and creating a culture of openness about mental health can lead to a more productive and engaged workforce. Workplace wellness is not just a corporate responsibility; it's an investment in the company's future. By prioritizing mental health, employers can create a more resilient and thriving workforce. This chapter underscores the importance of integrating mental health into the fabric of workplace culture, ensuring that employees feel supported and valued.

Chapter 10: Education and Prevention

Education and prevention are key components in the fight against mental health issues. This chapter delves into the role of mental health education in schools, the importance of early detection and intervention, and the impact of prevention programs and public health campaigns.

Mental Health Education in Schools:
Integrating mental health education into school curricula can equip students with the knowledge to understand and manage their mental health. For example, the "MindMatters" program in Australia provides schools with resources to implement a whole-school approach to mental health and well-being.

Early Detection and Intervention Strategies:

Early detection and intervention can prevent mental health issues from worsening. Programs like "Headspace" centers provide young people with access to mental health services, offering counseling, therapy, and support at the early stages of mental health difficulties.

Prevention Programs and Public Health Campaigns: Prevention programs aim to reduce the incidence of mental health conditions. The "Let's Talk" campaign by Bell Canada encourages open discussions about mental illness to break down stigma and promote early help-seeking behavior.

This chapter emphasizes the importance of education and prevention in fostering a proactive approach to mental health. By implementing these strategies, we can create a society that not only responds to mental illness but also actively works to prevent it, ensuring a healthier future for all.

Conclusion

As we reach the end of this journey, it's clear that mental health is an integral part of our overall well-being. This book has highlighted the multifaceted nature of mental health issues and the collective effort required to address them.

Summarizing Key Findings and Recommendations:
We've explored the importance of early detection, the impact of family support, the role of workplace wellness, and the power of education and prevention. The recommendations provided aim to strengthen these areas, advocating for increased funding, better access to care, and ongoing public education.

Mobilizing for Change: Steps Forward
For individuals, taking steps toward change means becoming informed, seeking help when needed, and supporting others. Communities can foster safe spaces for discussion and implement local initiatives. Policymakers must prioritize mental health in their agendas, ensuring that policies reflect the needs of those affected.

Envisioning a Future Where the Mind Truly Matters:

Imagine a future where mental health is not an afterthought but a central consideration in all aspects of life. A future where stigma is replaced with understanding, and where everyone has access to the care they need. This is the future we strive for—a future where the mind truly matters.

If you got value from this book, kindly drop a positive review for. You can also check out my other books here……

www.ingramcontent.com/pod-product-compliance
Lightning Source LLC
Chambersburg PA
CBHW012312240726
48656CB00008B/2651